Fishy Tales

OCT 15

Series Editor Deborah Lock
US Senior Editor Shannon Beatty
Editor Arpita Nath
Design Assistant Sadie Thomas
Art Editor Dheeraj Arora
Senior Art Editor Tory Gordon-Harris
Producer Christine Ni
Producer, Pre-production Siu Chan
Senior Producer, Pre-production Francesca Wardell
DTP Designers Almudena Díaz and Anita Yadav
Jacket Designer Natalie Godwin
Managing Editor Soma B. Chowdhury
Managing Art Editor Ahlawat Gunjan
Art Directors Rachel Foster and Martin Wilson

Reading Consultant
Linda Gambrell, Ph.D.
First American Edition, 2003
This edition, 2015
Published in the United States by DK Publishing
345 Hudson Street, New York, New York 10014

Copyright © 2003, 2009, 2015 Dorling Kindersley Limited
A Penguin Random House Company
15 16 17 18 19 10 9 8 7 6 5 4 3 2 1
001—271721—October/15

A catalog record for this book is available
from the Library of Congress.
ISBN: 978-1-4654-3494-4 (Paperback)
ISBN: 978-1-4654-3495-1 (Hardback)

DK books are available at special discounts when purchased in bulk for sales promotions,
premiums, fund-raising, or educational use. For details, contact:
DK Publishing Special Markets
345 Hudson Street, New York, New York 10014
SpecialSales@dk.com

Printed and bound in China.

The publisher would like to thank the following for their kind permission to reproduce their photographs:
(Key: a=above, b=below/bottom, c=center, l=left, r=right, t=top)
2-3 Getty Images: Pete Atkinson. **4 Science Photo Library:** GUSTO (l). **4-5 Getty Images:** Herwarth Voigtmann (t).
6-7 Getty Images: Jeff Hunter. **10 naturepl.com:** Alex Mustard (t). **10-11 OSF:** Tobias Bernhard. **12 Getty Images:** AEF
- Tony Malquist (t). **14-15 NHPA / Photoshot. 16-17 Corbis:** Stephen Frink. **18-19 Ardea. 20 Getty Images:** David
Fleetham (tl). **23 naturepl.com:** Constantino Petrinos (tr). **26-27 Corbis:** Jeffrey L. Rotman.
28 Getty Images: AEF - Tony Malquist (c). **30-31 Getty Images:** Jeff Hunter
Jacket credits: Front: Getty Images: Stuart Westmorland b. **iStockphoto.com:** cjp tc.
Back: Getty Images: Jeff Hunter / The Image Bank ca.

All other images © Dorling Kindersley
For further information see: www.dkimages.com

A WORLD OF IDEAS:
SEE ALL THERE IS TO KNOW

www.dk.com

Contents

Coral

Here is a coral reef.

What do you see?

coral

fish

Fish

eye

fin

6

spot

Small fish
swim in
and out of
the coral.

Turtles

The turtles play
in the ocean.

shell

flipper

Sea horses

tail

The sea horses
sway to and fro.

fin

snout

11

Starfish

arm

Starfish crawl
on the ocean floor.

Jellyfish

Jellyfish float
up and down
in the ocean.

tentacles

bell

15

Sharks

fin

tail

Here comes a shark.
It looks for food.

mouth

17

Octopuses

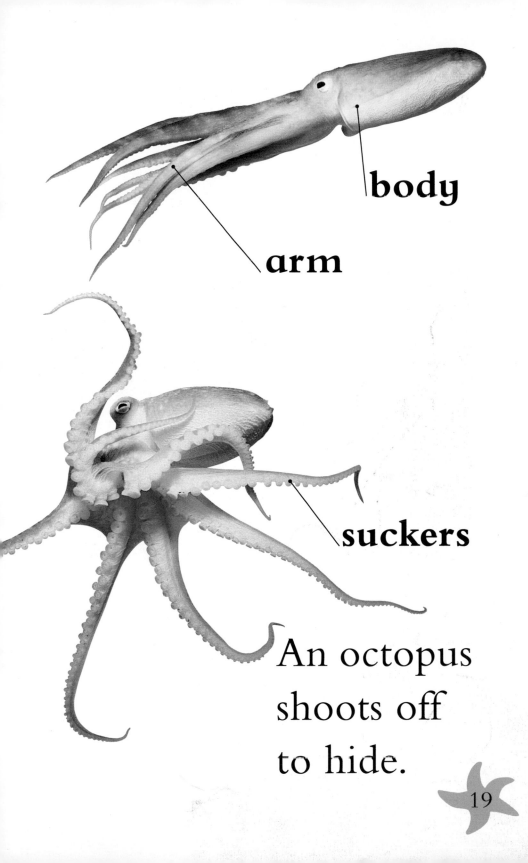

body

arm

suckers

An octopus
shoots off
to hide.

19

Crabs

claw

leg

Crabs hide in
the coral and
in big shells.

shell

21

Rays

tail

A ray hides on
the ocean floor.

eye

fin

23

Dolphins

A dolphin swims
away from
the shark.

mouth

tail

flipper

Eels

Eels look
out for
the shark.

tail

fin

eye

The shark swims away.

fin

gills

nose

Glossary

Eel
snakelike fish

Octopus
sea animal with eight long arms

Ray
flat fish with large winglike fins

Starfish
sea animal with five arms shaped like a star

Turtle
slow-moving reptile with a domed shell

Index

Have you read these other great books from DK?

LEARNING TO READ

Croak! Move in closer to look at the frogs and toads of the world!

Join the animals that wake up and search for food at night.

Find out about all types of weather from sunny days to thunderstorms.

BEGINNING TO READ

Roar! Thud! Meet the dinosaurs. Who do you think is the deadliest?

Splash! A young dolphin explores the ocean, diving and leaping.

Find out what happens on a farm through the seasons.